Henry Clinton

Narrative of the Campaign in 1781 in North America

Henry Clinton

Narrative of the Campaign in 1781 in North America

ISBN/EAN: 9783337425005

Printed in Europe, USA, Canada, Australia, Japan

Cover: Foto ©Suzi / pixelio.de

More available books at **www.hansebooks.com**

NARRATIVE

OF THE

CAMPAIGN IN 1781

IN

NORTH AMERICA.

BY

Sir HENRY CLINTON, K. B.

PHILADELPHIA:
JOHN CAMPBELL,
MDCCCLXV.

NARRATIVE

OF

LIEUTENANT-GENERAL

SIR HENRY CLINTON, K. B.

RELATIVE TO HIS

CONDUCT

DURING

PART OF HIS COMMAND OF THE KING's TROOPS

IN

NORTH AMERICA;

Particularly to that which refpects the unfortunate Iffue of the Campaign in 1781.

WITH AN

APPENDIX,

CONTAINING

Copies and Extracts of those Parts of his Correfpondence

WITH

LORD GEORGE GERMAIN,

EARL CORNWALLIS,

REAR ADMIRAL GRAVES, &c.

Which are referred to therein.

LONDON:

Printed for J. Debrett (fucceffor to Mr. Almon) oppofite Burlington-houfe, Piccadilly, 1783.

ERRATA.

	Page.	Line.
In the note,	8, -	3, *1781*, vice *1782*.
	13, -	12, *either*, vice *each*.
	24, -	19, *probably* before *be*, at the beginning of the line.
	46, -	16, *their*, vice *thus*.
	52, -	20, *&c.* after *accomplished*.

NARRATIVE

OF

LIEUTENANT GENERAL

Sir HENRY CLINTON, &c.

BEING conscious, that during my command in North America, my whole conduct was actuated by the most ardent zeal for the King's service, and the interests of the public, I was exceedingly mortified, when I returned to England, after a service of seven years in that country, to find that erroneous opinions had gone forth respecting it; and that many persons had, in consequence, admitted impressions to my prejudice.

duce. Anxious, therefore, to explain what had been misinterpreted or misrepresented, (as indeed might well be expected, from the publication of Lord C.'s letter of the 20th of October, without being accompanied by my answer to it) I had proposed taking an opportunity, in the House of Commons, of saying a few words on such parts of my conduct as seemed not to be sufficiently understood: and I flatter myself I should have been able to make it appear, that I acted up to the utmost of my powers, from the beginning to the end of my command; and that none of the misfortunes of the very unfortunate campaign of 1781 can, with the smallest degree of justice, be imputed to me.

But I arrived here so late in the session, that I was advised to defer it; and it was judged that the gracious reception I had just met with from my Sovereign rendered an immediate explanation unnecessary. I was

not,

not, however, apprifed to what degree the public prejudice had been excited againſt me elſe, I ſhould probably have been induced to have taken an earlier opportunity of offering to Parliament what I have to ſay on the ſubject. But the late change in public affairs, furniſhing ſo much more important matter for their deliberation, deprived me of the opportunity I thought I ſhould have had: and, as by the preſent receſs it is probable that I may not be able to execute my intentions before a late period, when perhaps peculiar circumſtances might force me through delicacy to decline it, I beg leave to lay before the public the following plain Narrative, which will, I truſt, remove prejudice and error.

I have much to regret that, when this buſineſs was diſcuſſed in the Houſe of Lords laſt ſeſſion of Parliament, the whole of my correſpondence, with the late American Miniſter, Lieutenant General Earl Cornwallis

wallis, and the Admirals commanding on the West-India and American stations, was not produced, or at least such parts thereof as, being necessary to explain my conduct, might have appeared consistently with state policy. Because the letters which compose that correspondence, being written to the moment as events happened, are certainly the most faithful records of my actions and intentions; and are consequently the clearest, fairest, and most unexceptionable testimonies I can adduce in their support. I hope, therefore, I shall stand exculpated from the necessity of the case, for any impropriety there may be in my annexing to this letter such of them as I may judge most requisite for that purpose. Three of them indeed will, I presume, be found very material, (Appendix No. IX.) as they contain my answers and observations upon Lord Cornwallis's letters of the 20th of October and 2d of December on the subject of the

the unfortunate conclusion of the last campaign in the Chesapeak;—which latter I am sorry to observe, were given to the public, while mine in answer were withheld from it;—I hope without design.

Although I never dared promise myself that any exertions of mine, with my very reduced force (nearly one-third less than that of my predecessor) could bring the war to a happy conclusion; yet I confess that the campaign of 1781 terminated very differently from what I once flattered myself it would; as may appear, by the subjoined extracts of letters, written in the beginning of that year,* and which were

trans-

---

* "I am most exceedingly concerned, my Lord, at the very unfortunate affair of the 17th of January, (Cowper's.) I confess I dread the consequences. But my hope is, as it ever will be, in your Lordship's abilities and exertions. I have much to lament, that Brigadier-general Arnold's projected move in favour of your Lordship's

transmitted to the Minister. I was led, however, into these hopes, more by the apparent distresses of the enemy than any material successes we had met with.

The plan I had formed for the campaign of 1781, (upon the expectation of a reinforcement

Lordship's operations will have been stopt by the appearance of the French ships. Discontent runs high in Connecticut. In short, my Lord, there seems little wanting to give a mortal stab to rebellion, but a proper reinforcement and a permanent superiority at sea for the next campaign; without which any enterprize depending on water movements must certainly run great risk. Until Colonel Bruce arrives, I am uncertain what reinforcements are intended for this army. The Minister has however assured me, that every possible exertion will be made."—Letter from Sir Henry Clinton to Lord Cornwallis, March 5, 1781.

"I cannot sufficiently express my extreme joy at reading Washington's letter. It is such a description of distress, as may serve to convince, that with a tolerable reinforcement from Europe, to enable your Excellency to determine on an offensive campaign, the year 1781 may

forcement from Europe—from the West-Indies—and from the Southward (after operation should cease in that quarter)—added to what I might be able to spare at the time from the small force under my immediate command at New-York) was calculated to make a fair and solid effort in favour of our friends—in a district where I had some reason to believe they were numerous and hearty; and where I judged it might be made with little danger, even from a temporary naval superiority of the enemy. This plan had been suggested to the Minister in the year 1780, and more particularly explained to him in 1781; notwithstanding which a preference was given to another, (Appendix, No. I.) which seemed to be forced

may probably prove the glorious period to your command in America, by putting an end to the rebellion."—Letter from Major-general Phillips to Sir H. Clinton, Portsmouth, Virginia, April 16, 1781.

forced (Appendix, No. II.) upon me by Lord Cornwallis's quitting the Carolinas, where I had left him in the command, and marching into Virginia; a measure, I must say, determined upon without my approbation, and very contrary to my wishes and intentions. The Minister directed me to support Lord Cornwallis and solid operation in Virginia; the danger of which, without a covering fleet, I had constantly represented to him. He repeatedly and positively promised me a covering fleet;* and when the Admiral

---

* Extracts from Lord George Germain's letters to Sir Henry Clinton:

April 4, 1782. "The lateness of the season will, I imagine, prevent Monf. De Grasse's undertaking any thing against the King's possessions in the West Indies. But it is probable, as soon as he has thrown supplies into the several islands, he will proceed to North America, and join the French forces at Rhode Island, and endeavour to revive the expiring cause of rebellion. But as Sir

Admiral arrived with the naval reinforcement from the Weſt-Indies, he was clearly of

Sir George Rodney's force is little inferior to his, and he will be watchful of his motions, I am not apprehenſive he will give him time to do you any material injury before he comes to your ſuccour."

May 2, 1781. "And as Sir George Rodney will bring you three more regiments from the Leeward Iſlands before the hurricane months, the augmentation of your force muſt, I ſhould think, be equal to the utmoſt of your wiſhes."

July 7, 1781. "The arrival of the reinforcement will, I hope, enable you to proceed immediately in the execution of your purpoſe, without waiting for the three regiments from the Weſt Indies; for I do not expect they will join you before the ſeaſon for offenſive operations there is over; when, I have reaſon to believe, the French fleet will puſh for North America, and Sir George Rodney will certainly follow them, to prevent them from giving you any interruption in your operations."

July 14, 1781. "The purpoſe of the enemy was long known here, and Sir George Rodney has been appriſed of it, and will certainly not loſe ſight of Monſ. De

of opinion himfelf, and of courfe convinced me, that he had brought that covering fleet. (Appendix, No. III.) Therefore, as Admiral Graves's fquadron was acknowledged to be fuperior to that under Monfieur de Barras, I could

De Graffe. The very proper ftep you took of tranfmitting him copies of the letters you had intercepted, muft confirm him in the refolution he had taken in confequence of the former intelligence. But as in a matter of fo great moment, no precaution fhould be omitted, or poffible contingency unguarded againft, extracts of the intercepted letters will be fent to him from hence, and precife inftructions given to him to proceed directly to North America, whenever Monf. De Graffe quits the Leeward Iflands."

July 24, 1781. "And I truft, that as Sir George Rodney knows De Graffe's deftination, and the French acknowledge his fhips fail better than their's, that he will get before him, and be in readinefs to receive him when he comes upon the coaft."

September 25, 1781. "I truft, before the end of Auguft, Sir Samuel Hood will have been with you, and that after his junction with Admiral Graves our fuperiority at fea will be preferved."

I could not but suppose that the arrival of Admiral Digby (hourly expected) would give us a most decisive naval superiority.—And here, perhaps, it may not be improper to remark, that though the Minister directs me, by his letters of the 2d of May, and 6th of June, to adopt solid operation in Virginia, he signifies to me his Majesty's approbation of my own plan, in a subsequent letter of the 14th of July, telling me at the same time, that "he has not the least doubt Lord "Cornwallis will have fully seen the rea- "sonableness of it, and has executed it with "his wonted ardor, intrepidity, and suc- "cess."

Under these circumstances, and with these assurances, I never could have the most distant idea that Mr. Washington had the least hopes of a superior French fleet in the Chesapeak; and I consequently never could suppose that he would venture to go there. But if he should, I was satisfied from the reasons already stated

stated, that I should be able to meet him there with every advantage on my side, by having the command of the waters of that bay—without which he could not possibly feed his army. This opinion has been also since confirmed by a letter from him to Count De Grasse, dated 26th of September 1781, (No. IV. Appendix) wherein he tells him, if he quits the Chesapeak, the enemy will certainly get possession of it, and he must disband his army.

Had my correspondence been produced, it would have appeared from it, and the returns accompanying it, that instead of seventeen, twenty, nay twenty-four thousand men, which it has been reported I had at New York (after the very ample reinforcements as the Minister acknowledges (No. V. Appendix) which I had sent to the southward) I had not 12,000 effectives, and of these not above 9,300 fit for duty, regulars and provincials. But had I had twice

twice that number, I do not know that, after leaving sufficient garrisons in the islands and posts depending (which it is admitted by all would take 6000) I could, as has been insinuated, have prevented the junction between Monsf. Rochambeau and General Washington, which was made in the highlands, at least 50 miles from me; or that I could have made any direct move against their army when joined (consisting then of at least 11,000 men, exclusive of militia, assembled on each side the Hudson) with any prospect of solid advantage from it. Or if I had as many reasons to believe that Mr. Washington would move his army into Virginia without a covering French fleet, as I had to think he would not; I could not have prevented his passing the Hudson under cover of his forts at Verplanks and Stoney Points. Nor (supposing I had boats properly manned) would it have been adviseable to have landed at Elizabeth town,

in

in the face of works which he might eafily have occupied (as they were only feven miles from his camp at Chatham) without fubjecting my army to be beat, *en detail.* Nor could I, when informed of his march towards the Delaware, have paffed an army in time to have made any impreffion upon him before he croffed that river. But with my reduced force, any attempt of the fort would have been madnefs and folly in the extreme.

With what might poffibly be fpared from fuch a force, nothing could be attempted except againft detachments from Mr. Wafhington's army, or (when reinforced in a fmall degree) againft fuch of it's diftant magazines as might occafionally happen to be unguarded. Two of the latter offered, one againft Philadelphia, which I certainly fhould have attempted in July, had Lord Cornwallis fpared me any part of 3000 men; but as his Lordfhip feemed to think he could

could not hold the stations we both thought eligible, if he spared me any part of the force with him, I was obliged to relinquish this design. The other much more important, was against Rhode Island. I had discovered by intercepted letters from all the French Admirals and Generals, that Count Rochambeau's army had marched from Rhode Island to join Mr. Washington at the White Plains; that their battering train and stores for siege were left at Providence under little more than a militia guard; and that their fleet remained in Rhode Island harbour with orders, as soon as repaired, to retire to Boston for security. By private information, which I had at that time, I found also that the works at Rhode Island were in a great measure dismantled, and had only a few invalids and militia to guard them, and that they were both there and at Providence under great apprehensions of a visit from us. From other motives as well as my own

knowledge

knowledge of thefe pofts, I had the ftrongeft reafon to expect the fulleft fuccefs to an attempt againft them, and I therefore immediately propofed to Admiral Graves a joint expedition for that purpofe; which he readily confented to. It was accordingly agreed between us, that it fhould be undertaken as foon as he could affemble his fleet, and a fmall reinforcement (hourly expected) fhould arrive from Europe. The reinforcement joined me on the 11th of Auguft, and the Admiral (who had failed on a cruife) having returned to the coaft on the 16th, I immediately renewed my propofal, (Appendix, No. VI.) The Admiral informed me in anfwer, that he was under the neceffity of fending the Robufte to the yard to be refitted, and that he fhould take the opportunity while that was doing of fhifting a maft or two in the Prudente; and when thofe repairs were accomplifhed, he would give me timely notice, (Appendix, No. VII.) The fhips were

were not ready on the 28th; Sir Samuel Hood, however, arriving on that day, I immediately ordered the troops to be embarked; and going to the Admirals on Long Iſland, I propoſed to them that the expedition ſhould inſtantly take place: but receiving intelligence that evening that Monſieur De Barras had ſailed on the 25th, it was of courſe ſtopped. Thus, to the Admirals great mortification and my own, was loſt an opportunity of making the moſt important attempt that had offered the whole war.

Early in September, to my great ſurpriſe, (for I ſtill conſidered our fleet as ſuperior) hearing that Mr. Waſhington was decidedly marching to the ſouthward, I called a council of all the general officers, who unanimouſly concurred with me in opinion, that the only way to ſuccour Earl Cornwallis was to go to him in the Cheſapeak.

Although I had every reaſon to diſapprove of Earl Cornwallis's march into Virginia, without consulting me, (at the risk of engaging me in dangerous operations, for which I was not prepared) yet, as I supposed he acted with at least the approbation of the Minister, I left him as free as air, when he arrived there, to plan and execute according to his discretion;—only recommending to him, in case he had none of his own, the plan I had offered to the Minister; which, notwithstanding the opinion given in the letter of July 14, before quoted,* I did not, however, find his Lordship

---

* Extract from Lord George Germain's letter to Sir Henry Clinton, July 14, 1781.—"It is with the most unfeigned pleasure I obey his Majesty's commands, in expressing to you his royal approbation of the plan you have adopted for prosecuting the war in the provinces south of the Delaware, and of the succours you have furnished, and the instructions you have given for carrying it into execution. The copies of the very important correspondence which so fortunately fell into your hands, (inclosed in your dispatch) shew the rebel affairs to be almost desperate, and that nothing but the success of

Lordship the least inclined to adopt. And that letter, which I did not receive till September, found me deeply and dangerously engaged in the operation he had forced me into.

And here, perhaps, it may be proper to give the reasons which induced me to recommend

of some extraordinary enterprize can give vigour and activity to their cause; and I confess I am well pleased that they have fixed upon New York as the object to be attempted, as I have not the least doubt but that the troops you had remaining with you, after the ample reinforcements you so judiciously sent to the Chesapeak, would be fully sufficient under your command to repel any force the enemy could bring against you. I cannot close this letter, without repeating to you the very great satisfaction your dispatch has given me; and my most entire and hearty coincidence with you in the plan you have proposed to Lord Cornwallis, for distressing the rebels, and recovering the southern provinces to the King's obedience. And as his Lordship, when he received your letters of the 8th and 11th of June, will have fully seen the reasonableness of it, I have not the least doubt but his Lordship has executed it with his wonted ardor, intrepidity, and success."

mend to Lord Cornwallis to secure a naval station for large ships, if one could be found that was capable of being fortified and maintained against a temporary superiority of the enemy at sea, agreeable to the instructions which I had before given to General Phillips, and which were of course to be now considered as such to his Lordship, (Appendix, No. X.)

Although I ought not to have apprehended that the enemy could have had a superiority at sea, after the assurances I had received from the Minister, I yet always wished to guard against even a possibility of it. Finding, therefore, by Lord Cornwallis's letters, that on his arrival in the Chesapeak, he had no plan of his own to propose, and that he did not incline to follow the one I had offered to his consideration, I recommended the taking a respectable defensive station either at Williamsburg, or York (the latter of which his Lordship

Lordſhip had informed me in a letter, dated 26th of May, he was inclined, from the reports which had been made to him, to think well of as a naval ſtation and place of arms) and left his Lordſhip at liberty to keep all the troops he had in Virginia, (amounting to about ſeven thouſand men). But thinking that he might well ſpare three thouſand; I deſired he would keep all that were neceſſary for a reſpectable defenſive, and deſultory water movements, and ſend me of three thouſand men all he could. His Lordſhip miſconceiving my intentions (as will, I truſt, be manifeſt to whoever reads our correſpondence) and conſidering my call for three thouſand men as unconditional, tells me that he could not with the remainder keep York and Gloucester; and that he ſhould, therefore, repaſs James-river and go to the ſtation at Portſmouth. Which reſolution (I confeſs) ſurpriſed me,

as

as he had a little before, in the letter above quoted, reprefented that poft as unhealthy, and requiring an army to defend it. On receipt of his Lordſhip's letter, I immediately confulted the Admiral, who was of of opinion, that a naval ſtation for large ſhips was abfolutely neceffary, and recommended Hampton-road. Therefore in my letter of the 11th July, I directed his Lordſhip to examine and fortify Old Point Comfort, which the Admiral and I thought would cover that Road, and in which there had been a fort for that purpofe for fifty years, though probably then in ruins. But his Lordſhip informing me in his letter of the 27th of July, that it was the opinion of the captains of the navy, the engineers, and himfelf, that any works erected on Old Point Comfort, "might "be eafily deftroyed by a fleet, and would "not anfwer the purpofe; and that there- "fore, according to the fpirit of my orders, "he "he should seize York and Gloucester, as "the only harbour in which he could hope "to be able to give effectual protection to "line of battle ships;" I supposed his Lordship had entirely approved of those posts; and that after examining them with the officers of the King's ships and his engineer, he would let me know if he should see reason to alter his opinion; and consequently I did not object to the choice he had made; nor indeed had I ever cause to do so before I saw his letter of the 11th of October, which I did not receive until the 16th, the day before he offered to capitulate, when for the first time I found his Lordship thought unfavourably of them. For on the 16th of August, his Lordship told me that he should apply to the Commodore for a ship to send me a state of things at York, and bring him back my commands; by which I was of course to understand that his Lordship would send me his own and the Commodore's opinion

nion of York and Gloucester, after his engineer had made a most exact survey, which he told me he was employed in, and of which I expected a copy, as his Lordship had before sent me of the one taken of Old Point Comfort. But not receiving these from his Lordship, I naturally concluded that the post of York and Gloucester was such as his Lordship and the Commodore approved; especially, as his Lordship, in his letter of the 22d of August, was pleased to say, "the "engineer has finished his survey and exa- "mination of this place, (York) and has "proposed his plan for fortifying it; which "appearing judicious, I have approved, and "directed to be executed." And in the same letter it was farther implied, that through the exertion of the troops, the works would be tolerably complete in about six weeks from that period: and from his saying also in the same letter, "I will not venture to
"take

"take any step that might retard the esta-
"blishing this post. But I request that your
"Excellency will please to decide whether
"it is most important for your plans, that a
"detachment of a thousand or twelve hun-
"dred men (which I think I can spare from
"every other purpose but that of labour)
"should be sent to you from hence, or that
"the whole of the troops here should con-
"tinue to be employed in expediting the
"works,") I naturally concluded that his
Lordship had not only sufficient to complete
his works by the time he mentioned, but that
he could spare that number from the defence
of them afterwards. His Lordship's letter of
the 29th of September moreover told me, "I
"have no doubt, if relief arrives in any reason-
"able time, that both York and Gloucester
"will be in possession of his Majesty's troops;"
and again, that of the 3d of October, "My
"works are in a better state of defence than
"we

"we had reason to hope." In short, I think his Lordship appears to have implied in all his letters, (except that of the 17th of September, the day he heard from Lieutenant Conway of the navy, that Monsf. De Grasse, by the junction of Monsieur de Barras, had thirty-five or thirty-six sail of the line) that he could hold out as long as his provisions lasted—which was, by his Lordship's own calculation, to the end of October at least.

From all these circumstances, I had flattered myself, that the works at York would have been tolerably complete by the 9th of October, the day Mr. Washington opened his batteries against them: and from the opinion given me by certain officers of rank, who had lately come from Lord Cornwallis at York, I was under no apprehensions for his Lordship before the latter end of that month; as I could not conceive that the enemy could possibly bring against him such a powerful a powerful battering train as would demolish his defences (such as I had reason to hope they would be) in so short a space of time as nine or ten days.

Although I never gave Lord Cornwallis assurances of the exertions of the navy before my letter of the 24th of September, when I did it in consequence of a council of war, composed of flag and general officers; I certainly never gave his Lordship the least reason to suppose they would not be made; as I always took it for granted, before Admiral Graves's letter to me of the 9th of September, that our fleet was superior to that of the enemy. Nor, indeed, did I know before I received Lord Cornwallis's letter of the 17th, (which was not until the 23d of September) that the enemy had thirty-six sail of the line, or that Monsieur de Barras had not already joined Monsieur de Grasse before the action of the 5th of September. But even against this superiority, great as it was, the Admirals were

were clearly of opinion, that a joint attempt should be made by us to succour the fleet and army in the Chesapeak. I certainly, therefore, never could have hinted to his Lordship that their exertions would not be made. The whole of this matter may, I think, be summed up as follows:

Lord Cornwallis's march into Virginia, without consulting his Commander in Chief, forced us into solid operation in that province. Being there, as his Lordship could not subsist his army without having a place of arms to cover his magazines, &c. &c. &c. it became absolutely necessary to fix on some healthy and respectable station, that could be made secure against a temporary superiority of the enemy at sea; and York and Gloucester seem to have been originally thought of by Lord Cornwallis, and approved by me for that purpose. But by his Lordship's misconceiving my orders, he quitted the Neck of York, and consequently relinquished every idea of occupying

pying thofe pofts. Soon afterwards, the Admiral thinking a naval ftation for large ships abfolutely neceffary, and recommending Hampton Road, I directed Lord Cornwallis to examine and fortify Old Point Comfort in James River; but his Lordfhip not approving of that ftation, made choice of York and Gloucefter.

I perfectly agree with Lord Cornwallis, that to abandon his pofts, after he had once fixed himfelf, (although by doing fo he might fave part of his army) would have been difgraceful, nay, perhaps fatal to our future profpects of eftablifhment in the Chefapeak, when fuch a meafure fhould be authorifed by a covering fleet. But even that misfortune, great as it may be reprefented, would have been preferable to the one which happened; and therefore I told his Lordfhip, in a converfation I had with him before I fent his letter of the 20th of October to be printed at New York, I had conceived hopes, that

that between the time of the French fleet's arriving in the Chesapeak, and his receiving information from me that Sir Samuel Hood had joined Mr. Graves, which was not until the 13th of September, or between that time and the junction of Mr. Washington with the Marquis De la Fayette, when his Lordship heard from Lieutenant Conway of the navy, that the enemy were thirty-six sail of the line, he would have tried to escape with part of his army to the southward; a step which certainly would have been justifiable, although in the conversation alluded to, his Lordship did not seem to think it would, unless I had given him assurances that the navy could not attempt to succour him; which assurances, however, I certainly could not possibly have given him.

If, therefore, Lord Cornwallis's letter of the 20th of October, giving an account of the unfortunate conclusion of the campaign, by the surrender of York Town, (Appendix, No.

No. VIII.) could ever have been underſtood to imply that the poſts of York and Gloucefter were not his Lordſhip's own choice, in preference to Old Point Comfort, which I had recommended to him; or that I had ever received information from his Lordſhip, that the ground at either was unfavourable, till the day before he had offered to capitulate; or that I had ever given him any aſſurances of the exertions of the navy, before my letter to him of the 24th of September, which he acknowledges he did not receive till the 29th; or that any aſſurances whatſoever given by me could have prevented his attacking the Marquis De la Fayette, before Mr. Waſhington joined that General, which was on the 27th of September; I am perſuaded it will appear that thoſe implications are not founded on any orders I gave his Lordſhip, and cannot be ſupported by any part of our correſpondence. And as I took an opportunity of telling his Lordſhip the ſame,

same, in a letter I sent him before he sailed from New-York, dated the 2d and 10th of December (which letter, however, did not appear when this part of our correspondence was produced before the House of Lords) I cannot doubt his Lordship is convinced that what I therein asserted is right.

Lord Cornwallis was pleased to tell me that his letter of the 20th of October, was written under great agitation of mind and in a great hurry. No man could possibly feel for his Lordship, and his dreadful situation, more than I did. And I will venture to say, no man could be more anxious, or would have gone greater lengths to succour him. Nor will this, I trust, be doubted, when it is recollected that the proposal first came from me for embarking six thousand men for that purpose on board an inferior fleet of twenty-seven sail of the line, including two fifties, to thirty-six; and thereby putting the fate of the American war on the joint exertions of

the

the fleet and army, to relieve that noble Lord and his gallant corps.

I have to lament that thefe exertions could not have been made in time. All the Admirals feemed of opinion at the council of war of the 24th September that there was every reafon to hope that the fleet would be ready to fail on the 5th of October. The troops intended for the expedition had been for fome time in readinefs to embark, and did actually do fo early in October. It feemed alfo to be the general opinion of the Admirals, that the enemy, although fuperior in number, could not obftruct the channel to York-river, fo as to prevent the paffage of our fleet, much lefs both paffages of the Chefapeak. Could the troops, which embarked under my immediate command, have been put on fhore on the Gloucefter fide, a junction with the part of Lord Cornwallis's corps on that fide was easy: but if they

E

they had been put on shore, even in James River, although a junction with his Lordship in York would have been scarcely practicable, it might have been made in some other part; or at least such diversions might have been made by the troops under my command as might have saved part of his Lordship's corps, (Appendix, No. XI.)

I must, therefore, repeat that I lament, and ever shall, that those exertions could not have been made in time. Because, from the professional merit of the Admirals who were to conduct us, and from the zeal which appeared so conspicuous when I proposed the move to them; and which, from their example was communicated to all ranks in the fleet; and with which, it is to be presumed, those of the army kept fully equal pace; I have every reason to think we should have had most complete success.

But at the same time, that truth compels

pels me to impute our misfortunes ultimately to the want of a covering fleet in the Chesapeak, I think it right to declare that, as a land officer, I do not feel myself a competent judge of the propriety and practicability of naval operations. Nor can I, as a servant of the State, entrusted with an important, but partial command, presume to enter into the counsel of Ministers; who, from a more elevated station, survey and balance the whole system of the campaign, and the general safety and welfare of the empire.*

Upon

---

* "I am, however, aware of the difficulties Administration must necessarily be exposed to, from the variety of important matters which demand its attention. And far be it from me, my Lord, to impute the delays I have experienced to any of the King's Ministers; but I cannot avoid lamenting that they do happen, and I tremble for the fatal consequences which may possibly some time or other ensue."—Sir Henry Clinton's letter to Lord George Germain, dated April 30, 1781.

Upon the whole, I am perfuaded, that had I been left to my own plans, and a proper confidence had been earlier repofed in me, the campaign of 1781 would not probably have ended unfortunately. But though that apparent want of confidence was at laft removed,* and the fulleft approbation I could wifh

* "The uneafinefs you exprefs on a certain occafion, muft have ceafed long before this reaches you, and, I truft, in full time to prevent your refigning the command to Earl Cornwallis. The meffage I fent you by Lieutenant-colonel Bruce was taken in writing to avoid any miftakes: for, as I was confcious of your having every reafon to be fatisfied with the protection fhewn to you by the King, and with the conftant defire of his Minifters to give you all poffible fupport, I could not help regretting that there fhould have been the leaft appearance of that want of confidence between us, which might prejudice the public fervice. Your explanation upon that fubject is perfectly fatisfactory; and you may depend upon finding every attention on my part to thofe requifitions which you may have occafion to make. The variety of fervices now carrying on in different parts of the world muft

account

wish given to the operations I had projected, my knowledge of the change happened too late to extricate me from the consequences of Lord Cornwallis's ill-fated march into Virginia, and the orders they had probably occasioned. Foreseeing many of the evils which would result from this fatal move the instant I heard of it, I immediately at the time communicated my apprehensions to the American Minister. And as my letter to him of the 18th of July, 1781, speaks very fully on this and other matters, of which I fear the public has been hitherto equally misinformed, I shall take the liberty to conclude this Narrative with the following extract from it:

"I can account for the disappointments you sometimes suffer. But you may rest assured, that every department of Government is anxious to furnish you with the most effectual means of carrying on the war with honour to yourself, and with advantage to the State."—Extract from Lord George Germain's Letter to Sir Henry Clinton, dated July 7th, 1781.

"I can say little more to your Lordship's sanguine hopes of the speedy reduction of the southern provinces, than to lament that the present state of the war there does not altogether promise so flattering an event. Many untoward incidents, of which your Lordship was not apprised, have thrown us too far back to be able to recover very soon, even what we have lately lost there. For if (as I have often before suggested) the good-will of the inhabitants is absolutely requisite to retain a country, after we have conquered it; I fear it will be sometime before we can recover the confidence of those in Carolina, as their past sufferings will of course make them cautious of publicly forwarding the King's interests before there is the strongest certainty of his army being in a condition to support them. I shall, therefore, most cordially join with your Lordship, in condemning the bad policy of taking possession of places at one time, and abandoning

ing them at another; and in the opinion that the war should be conducted upon a permanent and settled plan of conquest, by securing and preserving what has been recovered. But if these maxims have been, on any occasion, deviated from in the past progress of the war; I must, in justice to myself declare, that it has never been warranted by my orders, except, only in the case of Rhode-Island. This I doubt not will appear from the instructions I gave to General Leslie, and the other general officers, whom I sent on expeditions to the Chesapeak. For if Lord Cornwallis made a desultory move into North Carolina, and without a force sufficient to protect, or provisions to support them, invited by proclamation, the Loyalists to join him, and afterwards found it necessary to quit the friendly districts of that province, before he could have time to give them a fair trial, I am persuaded your Lordship will acknowledge

he

he did not act under my instructions:—nor were his Lordship's retreat to Wilmington, and subsequent move from thence to Virginia, in consequence of my orders: on the contrary, as I foresaw all the unhappy consequences of them, I should certainly have endeavoured to have stopt him, could I have known his intentions in proper time. But though his Lordship's movements, (which it must be confessed have been as rapid as your Lordship expected) have not to my sincere concern been successfully decisive; I am convinced he is, as I hope we all are, impressed with the absolute necessity of vigorous exertions in the service of his country at the present crisis. If mine, however, have not been equal to my inclinations, I have little doubt they will be found to be at least equal to my powers.

"I shall now, my Lord, beg leave to conclude with the strongest assurances, that no man can be more fervently desirous than I am am to fee an honourable end put to this moſt burthenſome war. And if I remain in the command, that no endeavours of mine ſhall be wanting to execute, in the fulleſt manner, the King's pleaſure and commands. Of the 10,000 men I ſolicited, only 4000 were even promiſed; and no portion of theſe, except a few recruits, has yet joined this part of the army. Your Lordſhip's laſt letters, however, give me hopes, that three Britiſh battalions and two thouſand ſix hundred German troops may be immediately expected. If all theſe arrive, I ſhall then be able, at a proper ſeaſon to reinforce the Cheſapeak corps very conſiderably; and if a reinforcement does not likewiſe come to the French armament already here, ſuch operations may be carried on as may perhaps produce ſome advantages in the courſe of the Winter. But if our reinforcement does not arrive, and the French ſhould receive theirs,

theirs, I think we shall have every thing to apprehend.

Before I close, however, I beg leave to say a word or two in explanation of two observations, in the Commissioners of Accounts Seventh Report; in order to obviate any implied censure, they may be supposed to point against me as Commander in Chief of the army in North America.

The Commissioners are pleased to say, "It appears that the number of the forces "decreased every year, from 1778, but the "issue for the extraordinary services of that "army greatly encreased, during the same "period."

And again, "In the account of the issues "to the officers in the four departments, "we find that the warrants issued to the "Quarter-master's-general, since the 16th "July 1780, and to the Barrack-master's- "general since the 29th June 1780, and to "the Commissaries-general, since the 25th
"of

"of May 1778, have been all temporary, for "sums on account; and that no final warrant "has been granted since those several periods. "So that these sums have been issued, with- "out even the ceremony of a quarterly "abstract, and the confidential reliance on "the officer, that his vouchers are forth "coming."

I arrived in London many days before the Commissioners of Accounts delivered in their Seventh Report to the House of Commons. Had those Gentlemen called upon me, as they did on Sir William Howe, and Lord Cornwallis; had they examined certain officers of the different departments, who arrived in England at the time I did, and who announced themselves to them; and had they read all the Reports of the different Boards of General Officers and Magistrates, that had been appointed by me at New York, to enquire into the expenditure of public money, (all which reports had been sent to the

Lords

Lords Commissioners of the Treasury many months before) I am persuaded that their Report would not have appeared on the table of the House of Commons in the shape it has done. For when they were informed (as they would have been by the means just stated) that all the rum purchased for the supply of the army during the whole period of my command, was paid for in America by my warrants, whereas before then it used to be paid for in England; that considerable sums of money were paid on my warrants for expences incurred during the command of my predecessor, which could not be brought to account sooner; that provisions to a very considerable amount were purchased in America, and paid for in America on my warrants, for the supply of the army, which might otherwise have been exposed to the greatest distress; all which together amounted to nearly 1,500,000l. and that the increase of posts, during my command, at Savannah,

Savannah, Charles Town, Cape Fear, Portsmouth, Penobscot, &c. requiring each their respective establishments, added of course to the extraordinaries of my army; and that, besides these, and many others which I could enumerate, the peculiar circumstances of my command exposed me to many expences unknown to my predecessor; it is presumed, those Gentlemen would have admitted, that the increase of the issues for the extraordinary services of the army under my command, was accounted for. This matter, however, went, by my desire, through a very full and formal investigation, in August 1781, before a Board of general officers and magistrates (of which Lieutenant-general Robertson was President) under the title of a Comparative View of Expences incurred, from the 31st December, 1775, to the 16th of May, 1778 (the time of Sir William Howe's command) and of what was paid by me, between the 26th of
May

May 1778, and the 31st of December 1780. Which produced the following report from that Board.

"The great national expence in the "first period of Sir William Howe's com-"mand, arose from the whole navy, and "a very numerous fleet of transports, be-"ing employed in attending the move-"ments of the army; no part of which "appears in Sir William Howe's war-"rants.

"The expence of the Quarter-master-"general, Barrack-master-general, and En-"gineer departments, were necessarily small, "while the troops were on board ships, or "had thus supplies from transports.

"During part of the first period, the "great article of expence, *rum*, was pro-"vided for by a contract made in Eng-"land, and paid for there. Whereas, du-"ring the second period, the rum was purchased

"chafed by the Commiffary-general, and
"paid for by the Commander in Chief's
"warrants. A very large quantity of pro-
"vifions purchafed alfo, during the latter
"period, fwells the amount of the war-
"rants.

"But what deftroys a poffibility of draw-
"ing any juft conclufion from a comparifon
"of the amount of the warrants in thefe
"two periods, arifes from this; that a great
"part of the expence incurred by Sir Wil-
"liam Howe, was paid by warrants granted
"by Sir Henry Clinton."

This report having been regularly tranf-
mitted to the Treafury, I muft fuppofe it
was laid before the Commiffioners of Accounts. Had it been read by thofe Gentlemen, it is prefumable it would have, at leaft,
accompanied theirs.

With regard to the fecond obfervation
alluded to, refpecting my not granting final
warrants to certain departments from certain
periods;

periods; if the commissioners had read all the above papers, I think it would have occurred to them; that as a Commissary of Accounts had been commissioned, and was actually employed in auditing the accounts of the different departments, I could not, with propriety, grant final warrants to any of the departments upon their quarterly abstracts (as had been before practised) untill their accounts had been first audited and certified by the Commissary.

As to the mode of supply which I found established, when I succeeded to the command of the army in North America, and which I understood had been approved by Government, I certainly could not, in prudence, have made any alterations or reduction in it, as long as I had offensive operation in view. The instant, however, that I received orders to place the army upon a strict defensive, I proposed such a reduction as could take place. And when I obtained

his

his Majesty's permission to resign the command, I recommended it to General Robertson, who was appointed to succeed me.

(Signed)

"H. CLINTON."

APPENDIX.

APPENDIX.

NUMBER I.

Extract of a Letter from Lord George Germain to Sir Henry Clinton, dated May 2, 1781.

"Conceiving therefore so highly as I do of the importance of the Southern provinces, and of the vast advantages which must attend the prosecution of the war upon the present plan of extending our conquests from south to north; it was a great mortification to me to find, by your instruction to Major-General Phillips, that it appeared to be your intention that only a part of the troops he carried with him should remain in the Chesapeak;

peak; and that he and General Arnold should return to New York, leaving only a sufficient force to serve for garrisons in the posts they might establish in Virginia. Your ideas, therefore, of the importance of recovering that province appearing to be so different from mine, I thought it proper to ask the advice of his Majesty's other servants upon the subject; and their opinions concurring entirely with mine, it has been submitted to the King; and I am commanded by his Majesty to acquaint you that the recovery of the Southern Provinces and the prosecution of the war, by pushing our conquests from south to north, is to be considered as the chief and principal object for the employment of all the forces under your command, which can be spared from the defence of the places in his Majesty's possession, until it is accomplished.

"The three regiments from Ireland, and the British recruits that went with them, are, I trust,

I truſt, well on their way by this time to Charles Town; and as Sir George Rodney will bring you three more regiments from the Leeward Iſlands before the hurricane months, the augmentation of your force muſt, I ſhould think, be equal to the utmoſt of your wiſhes.

NUMBER II.

Extract of a Letter from Lord George Germain to Sir Henry Clinton, dated June 6, 1781.

"I SHALL therefore only obſerve in addition to all I have hitherto written upon the the ſubject, that I am well pleaſed to find Lord Cornwallis's opinion entirely coincides with mine of the great importance of puſhing the war on the ſide of Virginia with all the force that can be ſpared until that province is reduced."

NUMBER III.

Copy of a Letter from Rear Admiral Sir S. Hood to Sir H. Clinton, dated off Cape Henry, August 25, 1781.

"SIR,

"HEREWITH you will receive a duplicate of the letter I had the honour to write you by Lieut. Delanoe of the Active brig, in case any misfortune should have befallen her in returning to New York. I am now steering for Cape Henry, in order to examine the Chesapeak. From thence I shall proceed to the Capes of the Delaware; and not seeing, or hearing any thing of De Grasse, or any detachment of ships he might have sent upon this coast, shall then make the best of my way off Sandy Hook. This I have communicated to Rear Admiral Graves, in order that he may determine my anchoring or not, as the King's service may require.

"I have

"I have the honour to fend you my line of battle, by which you will fee the number and force of his Majefty's fquadron under my command; and, I truft, you will think it equal, fully to defeat any defigns of the enemy, let De Graffe bring or fend what fhips he may, in aid to thofe under De Barras.

"I have the honour to be, &c.

(Signed) "SAM. HOOD."

NUMBER IV.

Copy of a Letter from General Wafhington to Count De Graffe, dated Williamfburg, September 26, 1781.

"I AM unable to defcribe to your Excellency the painful anxiety under which I have laboured fince the reception of the letter you did me the honour to write me of the 23d inftant. The motions of the naval force under your command, which your Excellency fays may poffibly happen, fince the information communicated

communicated to you by the Baron de Clozen, obliges me to point out the confequences that may follow; and warmly to urge a perseverance in the plan agreed upon between us. Permit me, in the first place, to repeat to your Excellency, that the attempt upon York, under the protection of your shipping, is as certain of success as a superior force and a superiority of measures can render any military operation; that the duration of the siege may be exactly ascertained; and that the capture of the British army is a matter so important in itself, and in its consequences, that it must greatly tend to bring an end to the war, and put our allied arms in certain possession of the most inestimable advantages.

"If your Excellency quits the Bay, an access is open to relieve York, of which the enemy will instantly avail themselves. The consequences of this will be not only the disgrace of abandoning a design on which are founded the fairest hopes of the allied forces, after

APPENDIX.

after a prodigious expence, fatigue, and exertions; but the probable difbanding of the whole army; for the prefent feat of war being fuch, as abfolutely precludes the ufe of waggons, from the great number of large rivers which interfect the country, there will be a total want of provifions, unlefs this inconvenience is remedied by water carriage. This province has been fo exhaufted by the ravages of the enemy, and by the support already given to our forces, that fubfiftence muft be drawn from a diftance, and that can be done only by a fleet fuperior in the Bay.

"I earneftly beg your Excellency would confider, that if, by moving your fleet from the fituation agreed on, we lofe the prefent opportunity, we fhall never hereafter have it in our power to ftrike fo decifive a ftroke, that the Britifh will labour without intermiffion to fortify a place fo useful to their fhipping; and that then the period of an honourable peace will be farther diftant than ever.

"The

"The confidence I have in your Excellency's manly spirit and naval talents leaves me no doubt that the consideration of the consequences that must follow your departure from the Bay will determine you to use all possible means for the good of the common cause. From the assurances of the most expert sailors, I am persuaded that your Excellency may take such a position in the Bay as to leave nothing to be apprehended from an attempt of the English fleet; that this position will at the same time facilitate the operations of the siege, secure the transportation of our provisions by water, and accellerate our approaches by landing our heavy artillery and warlike necessaries in York River almost close to our trenches.

"The force said to have arrived under Admiral Digby, as the news comes from the British themselves, may not only be exaggerated, but perhaps absolutely false; but supposing it to be true, their whole force united cannot be such as to give them any hopes of success

success in the attacking your fleet. If the position for your ships to lie at an anchor, which we agreed upon, has since appeared impracticable, there is still another measure may be adopted; which, though much inferior as to the security and facility it will give to our land operations, may still be of advantage to our affairs. The measure, I mean, is to cruise off the Bay, so as to keep the Capes always in sight, and to prevent any English vessels getting in.

"Whatever plan you may adopt, I am to press your Excellency to persevere in the scheme so happily concerted between us; but if you should find insurmountable obstacles in the way, let me ultimately beg of you not to relinquish the last mentioned alternative of preventing all vessels from the enemy entering the Bay of Chesapeak.

"The British Admiral may manœuvre his fleet, and endeavour to draw you from the main object we have in view; but I can never

never believe, that he will seriously wish to bring on a general action with a fleet, whose force, I will answer for it, is superior to the most exaggerated accounts we have of theirs. Passed experience has taught them not to hazard themselves with equal numbers; and has drawn from them, though unwillingly, the most respectful opinions of their enemy.

"Permit me to add that the absence of your fleet from the Bay may frustrate our design upon the garrison at York. For in the present situation of matters, Lord Cornwallis might evacuate the place with the loss of his artillery, baggage, and a few men, sacrifices; which would be highly justifiable from the desire of saving the body of the army.

"The Marquis de la Fayette, who does me the honour to carry this letter to your Excellency, will explain to you better than any other person, or than I can do by letter, many particulars of our present position. Your Excellency is acquainted with his candour and talents,

APPENDIX. 61

talents, which entitles him to your confidence I have ordered him not to pafs the Cape for fear of accident, in cafe you fhould be at fea. If this be fo, he will inclofe this difpatch in a letter from himfelf,

"I have the honour, &c.

"G. WASHINGTON."

NUMBER V.

Extract from Lord George Germain's Letter to Sir Henry Clinton, dated October 12, 1781.

"IT is a great fatisfaction to me to find your ideas of the importance of fecuring a naval ftation in the Chefapeak capable of giving protection to the King's fhips, appointed to intercept the navigation of that Bay, fo entirely coincided with my own; and that the plan you had concerted for conducting the military operations in that quarter
corresponds

corresponds with what I had suggested in my former letters to you on that subject. I trust, therefore that Lord Cornwallis will retain the whole of the troops you so very properly spared for the service in the Chesapeak: or if he has sent you any part, that you will return them to him. And as soon as the heats are abated, transport a strong detachment to Baltimore, &c.

"The provision you made for the southern service was certainly most ample. And I have always considered and spoke of it as a circumstance highly to your honour; and as an evidence of your being actuated by the purest zeal for the public service. And though I lament exceedingly that from a concurrence of untoward events, the success was not equal to the sanguine expectations I had entertained, I never imputed any part of the disappointment to a deficiency in your supplies."

APPENDIX. 63

NUMBER VI.

Extract from Sir Henry Clinton's Letter to Rear-Admiral Graves, dated August 16, 1781.

"I CANNOT say I credit the reports of the French being upon the coast. Should they prove false, and there was little probability of their coming for a week or ten days, I think those could not be better employed than in a visit to Rhode-Island. The recruits I have lately received enable me to make this offer, whenever you think it prudent to attempt it. If you determine, I request that Captain Duncan may direct the water-movements of the army."

Extract from Sir Henry Clinton's Letter to Rear-Admiral Graves, dated August 18, 1781.

"WHENEVER, Sir, you think the fleet under your command is in number and state equal

equal to the undertaking, and you will give me twenty-four hours notice, every thing shall be immediately embarked; and I shall with pleasure accompany you myself on it."

NUMBER VII.

Extracts from Rear-Admiral Graves's Letters to Sir H. Clinton, dated 18 *and* 21 *August,* 1781.

"IN answer to your proposition, I can only assure you by letter, what I had the honour to declare in person, that I am ready to concur with your Excellency in any enterprize where you found a probability of success; and that I would risk the squadron whenever you thought it adviseable to risk the army.

"The Robuste is so leaky, I am forced to send her to the yard for reparation; and I suspect that her guns and heavy furniture must be taken out to enable the shipwrights to

APPENDIX. 65

to examine as much of her bottom as poffible. Whilft that is doing, the Prudent will change one of her mafts, if not two. By this ftate you will fee our naval capacity. 21 Auguft, 1781. How foon the Robufte will be ready is yet impoffible to form a judgement upon, as we cannot yet learn the extent of her defects. The Prudent will, I am confident, be ready in much lefs time; and fo will all the other fhips, I have not a doubt.

"Your Excellency may reft affured that timely notice fhall be given, and as early as poffible to determine upon the day the fquadron will be fit to act; for I would not wifh that a fingle day fhould be loft."

NUMBER VIII.

Extract from Lord Cornwallis's Letter to Sir H. Clinton. York Town, Virginia, 20 October, 1781.

"I HAVE the mortification to inform your Excellency, that I have been forced to give

give up the posts of York and Gloucester, and to surrender the troops under my command, by capitulation, on the 19th instant, as prisoners of war to the combined forces of America and France.

"I never saw this post in a favourable light. But, when I found I was to be attacked in it, in so unprepared a state, by so powerful an army and artillery, nothing but the hopes of relief would have induced me to attempt its defence. For I would either have endeavoured to escape to New York, by rapid marches from the Gloucester side, immediately on the arrival of General Washington's troops at Williamsburg; or I would, notwithstanding the disparity of numbers, have attacked them in the open field, where it might have been just possible that Fortune would have favoured the gallantry of the handful of troops under my command. But, being assured by your Excellency's letters that every possible means would be tried, by the navy and

and army, to relieve us, I could not think myself at liberty to venture on either of those desperate attempts. Therefore, after remaining two days in a strong position, in front of this place, in hopes of being attacked, upon observing that the enemy were taking measures which could not fail of turning my left flank in a short time; and receiving, the second evening, your letter of the 24th September, informing me that the relief would fail about the 5th of October, I withdrew within the works on the night of the 29th of September, hoping, by the labour and firmness of the troops, to protract the defence until you could arrive. Every thing was to be expected from the firmness of the troops. But every disadvantage attended their labour; as the works were to be continued under the enemy's fire; and our stock of intrenching-tools, which did not much exceed four hundred when we began to work in the latter end of August, was now much diminished.

"A

"A succefsful defence, however, in our situation, was perhaps impossible; for the place could only be reckoned an intrenched camp, subject in most places to enfilade; and the ground in general so disadvantageous, that nothing but the necessity of fortifying it as a post to protect the navy could have induced any person to erect works upon it."

Copy of a Letter from Sir Henry Clinton to Earl Cornwallis, dated 30 *November,* 1781.

[This letter was not produced in the House of Lords.]

"My Lord,

"AFTER the conversation I had with your Lordship before I sent your letter to be published, in which we seemed so perfectly to agree, I must beg your Lordship's pardon for again troubling you on the subject. But, being informed, perhaps officiously, that some people here suppose there are passages in that letter

letter which convey an idea that you had been compelled by my orders to take the poſt of York, (though it was not your own preference;) that you had repreſented the defects of the ground; and were detained there contrary to your own judgement;—and likewiſe that I had promiſed the exertions of the navy before my letter of the 24th of September: I am perſuaded your Lordſhip will readily excuſe my requeſting a more formal avowal of your ſentiments, leſt I ſhould have then miſtaken them. Becauſe, if that ſhould unfortunately be the case, I may perhaps be under the neceſſity of taking meaſures to obviate your letter being viewed in the ſame light in England.

"I have the honour, &c.

"H. CLINTON."

NUMBER IX.

Copy of Earl Cornwallis's Letter to Sir Henry Clinton, dated New York, 2d December, 1781.

[This letter was read in the House of Lords.]

"SIR,

"YESTERDAY afternoon I was honoured with your Excellency's letter of the 30th of November.

"I do not recollect that any conversation passed between us the other day, before the publication of my letter, relative to my reasons for taking possession of the posts of York and Gloucester. But, in my answers to your dispatches, dated the 8th and 11th of July, directing me so positively to possess a harbour in the Chesapeak for line of battle ships, your Excellency will see, that, after finding that works on Point Comfort could not protect a naval

naval force in Hampton Road, I thought that I acted in strict obedience to your orders by taking possession of those posts. I thought it unnecessary to enter into a minute detail of the disadvantages of the ground, either on my first examination of it in the month of June, or on my return to it in August; because, on the first occasion, as I have already had the honour of explaining to your Excellency, I did not, after seeing it, entertain for a moment an idea of occupying it, not thinking myself at liberty, by the instructions under which I then acted, to detain the greater part of the force in Virginia for the purpose of securing a harbour for ships of the line; and, on my return to it in August, I thought it then became my duty to make the best of it I could, having no other harbour to propose in its place.

"In regard to the promise of the exertions of the navy previous to your letter of the 24th of September, I can only repeat what I had

the

the honour of saying to your Excellency in the conversation to which you allude; that, without any particular engagement for the navy before that date, all your letters held out uniformly hopes of relief; and that I had no reason, from any of them, to suppose that you had lost sight of the possibility of effecting it. And that, under those hopes, after serious reflection, I did not think that it would have been justifiable in me to abandon those posts, with our numerous sick, artillery, stores, and shipping; or to risk an action, which, in all probability, would in its consequences have precipitated the loss of them.

"My letter from York, dated the 20th of October, was written under great agitation of mind and in great hurry, being constantly interrupted by numbers of people coming upon business or ceremony. But my intention in writing that letter was to explain the motives that influenced my own conduct, and to narrate

rate the incidents that preceded the extremity that forced us to furrender.

"I have the honour, &c.

"CORNWALLIS."

NUMBER IX.

Copy of a Letter from Sir Henry Clinton to Earl Cornwallis, dated New York, 2d and 10th December, 1781.

[This letter was not read in the House of Lords.]

"My Lord,

"AS your Lordfhip is pleafed, in your letter of this day, to revert to the circumftance of your quitting Williamfburg Neck and repaffing the James River, fo contrary to the intentions I wifhed to exprefs in my letters of the 11th and 15th of June, and thofe referred to by them, and which I thought they would have clearly explained. Your Lordfhip will, I hope, forgive me, if I once more repeat that I am am of opinion, if those letters had been properly understood by your Lordship, you would at least have hesitated before you adopted that measure. For I humbly presume it will appear, upon a re-perusal of them, that it was my desire to recommend to your Lordship the taking a healthy defensive station, either at Williamsburg or York; and, after keeping what troops you might want for the ample defence of such a post, and desultory movements by water, to send me such a proportion of the corps (mentioned in a list) as you could spare, taking them in the succession they are there placed. Your Lordship, on the contrary, understood these as conveying a positive order to send me three thousand men, (by which you say your force would have been reduced to about two thousand four hundred rank and file fit for duty;—having, it is presumed, above 1500 sick;) and was pleased to tell me, in your answer, that you could not, consistent with my plans, make safe defensive posts

posts at York and Gloucester, (both of which would be necessary for the protection of shipping;) and that you should immediately repass James River, and take measures for complying with my requisition.

"I own, my Lord, that my opinion of the obvious meaning of the letters referred to, continues still the same; and I am exceedingly sorry to find, by the letter you have now honoured me with, that it differs so widely from your Lordship's. It is plain, however, we cannot both be in the right.

"My letter of the 11th of July directs your Lordship to fortify Old Point Comfort, in the mouth of James River, with the intention of securing Hampton Road, which the Admiral recommended as the best naval station, and requested I would occupy. But your Lordship's letter of the 27th of July informs me, you had examined Old Point Comfort, with the officers of the navy, and the engineers, and that you were all of opinion, a post there

there would not anfwer the purpofe; and that you fhould, therefore, in compliance with the *fpirit* of my orders, feize York and Gloucefter, being the only harbour in which you could hope to be able to give *effectual protection* to line of battle fhips. Suppofing, therefore, of courfe, that your Lordfhip approved, in every refpect, of York and Gloucefter, from the preference you had thus given them to the poft I had recommended, I did not oppofe the choice you had made; having never received the leaft hint from your Lordfhip that the *ground* of York was unfavourable, or liable to be enfiladed till after you had capitulated.

"With refpect to your Lordfhip's having been influenced in your conduct, by the hopes of relief, (which you fay was uniformly held out to you in all my letters) your Lordfhip cannot be infenfible, that the poffibility of effecting it muft have entirely depended upon the exertions of the navy; which, as I was

not

not authorised to promise before the 24th of September, I am persuaded your Lordship will readily acknowledge, that if your letter of the 20th October implies I had done so before that period, the implication cannot be supported by any thing I wrote previous to my letter of that date, which you received on the 29th.

"As, therefore, my letters of the 2d and 6th of September, which promise only my own exertions, did not reach your Lordship before the 13th and 14th of that month, and you did not before then know of Sir Samuel Hood's arrival, or of Mr. Graves's having more than seven sail of the line to combat Monsieur De Grasse's force, which on the 29th of August you had heard consisted of at least twenty-five sail of the line; your Lordship consequently could have no hopes of relief before that time. And with respect to your escape to New-York, immediately on the arrival of General Washington's troops at Williamsburg,

Williamsburg, which your letter of the 20th of October implies you were prevented from undertaking, by the receipt of mine of the 24th of September; I must beg leave to observe, that if it had been ever practicable after the time your Lordship mentions (which I am free to own I do not think it was) it must have been between that period and the time of the enemy's force appearing before your lines. It may, therefore, be presumed, you could not have been prevented by any thing I said in that letter, as you did not receive it until after the latter event took place. But I readily admit, my Lord, that none of my letters could give you the least reason to suppose that an attempt would not be made to succour you.

"Your Lordship will, I am persuaded, also forgive me, if I again take notice of the too positive manner in which you are pleased to speak of the opinion I gave you about the failing of the fleet; as my words were, "there is "is every reason to hope we shall start from "hence *about* the 5th of October." And in my letter of the next day, for fear that should appear too positive, I say, "It is supposed "the necessary repairs of the fleet will detain "us here to the 5th of next month; and your "Lordship must be sensible that unforeseen "accidents may lengthen it out a day or two "longer."

With regard to entrenching tools, the want of which your Lordship so much complains of, I can only say, that by the returns made to me by the Adjutant-general, it appears that two thousand five hundred had been sent to the Chesapeak by the Engineer, since General Arnold's expedition, inclusive; and that the first moment a requisition was made for more, (which was not before the 23d of August) I ordered an additional supply to be sent, which were prevented from going, by the arrival of the French fleet. I own, however, that I was not at that time very uneasy on this score, as

I sup-

I supposed it possible for your Lordship to have collected a sufficiency from the neighbouring plantations any time before the investiture was begun.

"December 10.——I had wrote thus far, my Lord, immediately after the receipt of your Lordship's letter of the 2d instant. But considering that it was possible you might not have adverted to the implications, which your letter of the 20th of October may be thought to bear, from the great agitation of mind and hurry in which you tell me it was written, I was unwilling to give you at that time more trouble on the subject;—in the honest hope that your Lordship's candour will induce you most formally to disavow your having any such intentions by writing that letter, in case you find, on your arrival in England, that the passages of it (which I have taken notice of) are understood as I suspect they may be. And I therefore intended to have sent this letter to a friend to be delivered to you in London,

APPENDIX.

London; but upon confidering your letter of the 2d inftant, (which I have had more leifure to do fince my public difpatches were clofed) I am of opinion, that it is properer your Lordfhip fhould receive my anfwer to it here.

"I have the honour, &c.

(Signed) "H. CLINTON."

"P. S. Having forgot to fpeak to the part of your Lordfhip's letter of the 2d inftant, where you fay, 'I do not recollect that any 'converfation paffed between us the other 'day, before the publication of my letter, 'relative to my reafons for taking poffeffion 'of the the pofts of York and Gloucefter,' I beg leave to do it here.

"It is true, my Lord, no converfation paffed from your Lordfhip on that fubject. But when, in the converfation alluded to, I mentioned that I had directed you to examine Old Point Comfort, and fortify it, but that, difapproving of that poft, you had feized York,

York, and that therefore York was your Lordship's preference; as you were pleased not to make me any answer, I took it for granted you agreed with me.

"H. CLINTON.

"Lieutenant-general
"Earl Cornwallis."

NUMBER IX.

Extract of a Letter from Sir Henry Clinton, to Lord George Germaine, dated December 3, 1781.

"YOUR Lordship will have received in my Dispatch, No. 146, the copies of Lord Cornwallis's letter to me of the 20th of October, his capitulation for the posts of York and Gloucester, and the other papers which accompanied it. But your Lordship will perceive, that I declined making any remarks upon his letter until I saw his Lordship; knowing that my whole correspondence with him being in your Lordship's possession, every thing

thing which wanted explanation could readily be cleared up. His Lordship having arrived here on the 19th ultimo, I have had several conversations with him; and I have now the honour to inclose, for your Lordship's information, the copy of a letter I wrote him on the subject, with his Lordship's answer.

"I perceive by Lord Cornwallis's letter of the 20th of October, that his opinion of the post of York is very unfavourable; and he since tells me, that he does not think the enemy will be able to make a strong one of it. Had his Lordship, however, not been so very decided in his sentiments of the post, all the accounts I had ever before received of the situation and defensibility of the ground would, I confess, have inclined me to have thought well of it."

NUMBER IX.

Copy of a Letter from Sir Henry Clinton, to Lord George Germain, dated December 6, 1781.

"My Lord,

"I have so often had the honour of delivering the same sentiments to your Lordship, that I must beg your pardon for again troubling you with the repetition, that I have ever been of opinion that operation should not be undertaken in the Chesapeak, without having a naval superiority in these seas; and to the want of it, and perhaps to that alone, are we to impute our late misfortune in that quarter. Therefore, when I did myself the honour of sending you a copy of Lord Cornwallis's letter to me of the 20th of October, I did not think it necessary to trouble your Lordship with any remarks upon some passages of it, which might seem to imply, that his Lordship had been

APPENDIX. 85

been forced into a bad poft by my orders, notwithftanding he had reprefented its defects, and had been induced to remain there contrary to his judgment by the pofitive affurances I had given him of relief; efpecially as your Lordfhip was poffeffed of our correfpondence, which could in the fulleft manner invalidate every implication of that fort, and I wifhed to have an opportunity of fpeaking to Lord Cornwallis before I faid any thing on fo delicate a fubject.

"Since Lord Cornwallis's arrival here, I have had a good deal of converfation with his Lordfhip upon this bufinefs; by which, and by the anfwer he has fent me to a letter I wrote him thereon, (copies of which are inclofed) it appears, that his Lordfhip admits this was not the cafe. But as Lord Cornwallis's difavowal is not fo explicit and direct in his letter, as I could wifh, and I think juftice to my character requires, I beg your Lordfhip's attention to the following obfervations;
which

which I hope the anxiety I must naturally feel on this occasion, will plead my excuse for troubling you with; though they may not be necessary to vindicate me with your Lordship, who is already so competent to judge.

"I am persuaded that it will appear by my letters to Lord Cornwallis of the 11th and 15th of June, and those referred to by them, that I recommended his taking a healthy, defensive station, either at Williamsburg, or York; and desired that, after keeping what troops he might want for its most ample defence and desultory movements by water, his Lordship would send me such a proportion of the corps (mentioned in a list) as he could spare, taking them in the succession they are there placed. But his Lordship, on the contrary, understanding that these letters conveyed a positive order to send me three thousand men, (by which he says his force would have been reduced to about two

two thousand four hundred rank and file fit for duty, having probably at that time a numerous sick) told me in his answer, that he could not, consistent with my plans, make safe defensive posts at York and Gloucester, (both which would be necessary for the protection of shipping) and that he should immediately repass James River, and take measures for complying with my requisition. Finding, therefore, that his Lordship had so entirely misconceived my intentions, I immediately consulted with Rear Admiral Graves upon the subject of his letter; and the Admiral being of opinion that a naval station in Chesapeak for large ships was absolutely requisite, and that Hampton Road appeared to be the fittest for the purpose, I desired his Lordship, at the Admiral's request, to examine Old Point Comfort in the mouth of James River, and fortify it, upon the supposition that a work there would secure that harbour;

harbour; and if his Lordship thought a post at York necessary to cover Old Point Comfort, he was at liberty to take that also. This order was sent to Lord Cornwallis in my letter of the 11th of July, and his Lordship's answer to it is dated the 27th; wherein he informs me, that having examined Old Point Comfort with the Captains of the King's ships and the engineers, and being all of opinion a post there would not answer the purpose, he should, in compliance with the spirit of my orders, seize York and Gloucester, being the only harbour in which he could hope to be able to give effectual protection to line of battle ships. Copies of these letters are inclosed for your Lordship to refer to; and I trust it will appear from them, that the post at York was in this instance entirely his Lordship's choice. But never having received any representation from his Lordship, by which I could have

the

the least conception he thought the ground disadvantageous and liable to enfilade, (as stated in his letter of the 20th of October) and, supposing from the preference his Lordship had thus given it to the one I had recommended, that he fully approved of York and Gloucester, I own I did not oppose his laying hold of them, as I could not entertain the smallest doubt of their being defensible, and such a post as I had told his Lordship I wanted. And, indeed, if his Lordship had not now informed me that it was a bad one, the eagerness with which I understand the French have since seized and are fortifying it, would incline me still to think well of it.

"With respect to his Lordship having been influenced in his conduct by the hopes of relief, (which he is pleased to say I uniformly held out to him in all my letters) his Lordship could not be insensible that the possibility of effecting it must have entirely depended upon the exertions of the fleet, which, as I was not authorized to promise him before the council of war held on the 24th of September, I am persuaded that the implication in his Lordship's letter that I had done so before that period, cannot be supported (as indeed his Lordship now seems to acknowledge) by any thing I wrote to him, previous to my letter of that date, which he received on the 29th. As, therefore, my letters of the 2d and 6th of September, which promise only my own exertions, did not reach his Lordship before the 13th and 14th of that month, and he did not before then know of Sir S. Hood's arrival, or that Admiral Graves had more than seven sail of the line to combat Monsieur de Grasse's force, whose arrival, it appears from his Lordship's letters, he knew of on the 29th of August, and supposed it to be twenty-five sail of the line, his Lordship

ship consequently did not receive from me any hopes of relief before that time.

"With regard to his Lordship's escape to New York, immediately on the arrival of General Washington's troops at Williamsburg, which his letter of the 20th of October implies he was prevented from undertaking by the receipt of mine of the 24th of Sept. I cannot help being of opinion, that a retreat, after Mr. Washington joined, was impracticable, and that it was at no time to be effected to the northward, for reasons which I gave his Lordship. But had it been ever possible, after the time his Lordship mentions, it must, I think, have been between that period and the time of the enemy's force presenting itself before the lines of York; and it is consequently presumable, his Lordship was not prevented by any thing I said in that letter, as he acknowledges he did not receive it until after the latter event took place. But I readily admit, my Lord, that

none

none of my letters could give his Lordship the least reason to suppose that an attempt would not be made to succour him, though, I must confess, I think his Lordship speaks in his letter rather too positively of the opinion I gave in mine, as to the time of the fleet's sailing. My words being, 'There is 'every reason to hope we shall start from 'hence about the 5th of October.' And left even that should be thought positive, I the next day told him, 'that unforeseen 'accidents may lengthen it out a day or two 'longer.'

"The complaint his Lordship makes of the want of intrenching tools, I can only answer, by saying, that it appears from the Adjutant-general's returns to me, that two thousand five hundred had been sent by the engineer to the Chesapeak with the different expeditions, since the one commanded by General Arnold inclusive; and the first moment a requisition was made for more (which

was

was not before his Lordship's letter of the 22d of August) I ordered an additional supply to be sent, which were prevented from going by the arrival of the French fleet. But I must own, my Lord, that I was not then very uneasy on this score, as I flattered myself it was possible for his Lordship to have collected what he wanted from the neighbouring plantations any time before the investiture was begun.

"No man, my Lord, can feel more sensibly than I did for the unhappy situation of Lord Cornwallis and his gallant army, whose meritorious conduct, spirit, and zeal, on all occasions, must heighten our anxiety and concern for their present fate; and therefore as his Lordship is pleased to tell me that his letter of the 20th of October was written under great agitation of mind and in great hurry, which might possibly have prevented his adverting to the implications which it may be thought to bear, I cannot, at present,
wish

wish to give his Lordship more trouble on the subject, although his answer of the 2d instant is not so explicitly satisfactory as I expected it would have been; for, if the passages in that letter, which I have taken notice of, should be understood in Europe in any respect to my prejudice, I cannot doubt his Lordship will have candour enough most formally to disavow his having any such intentions. But if his Lordship, contrary to my expectation, shall not be inclined to do so, I must be obliged, though reluctantly, most earnestly to request your Lordship to render me that justice, (which I am persuaded you think I deserve) by publishing this letter.

"I have the honour, &c.

"H. CLINTON."

NUMBER X.

Extract from Sir H. Clinton's Instructions to Major-General Philips, dated March 10, 1781.

"IF the Admiral disapproving of Portsmouth, and requiring a fortified station for large ships in the Chesapeak, should propose York Town, or Old Point Comfort, if possession of either can be acquired and maintained without great risk or loss, you are at liberty to take possession thereof. But if the objections are such as you think forcible, you must, after stating those objections, decline it till solid operations take place in the Chesapeak."

Extract

Extract from the Substance of Conversations held with General Philips, sent to that General Officer for his Guidance.

"BUT if the heights of York, and those on the Gloucester side, cannot be so well and so soon fortified as to render that post *hors d'insult* before the enemy can move a force, &c. against it, it may not be adviseable to attempt it. In that case something may possibly be done at Old Point Comfort to cover large ships lying in Hampton road, which is reckoned a good one. If neither can be secured, we must content ourselves with keeping the Chesapeak, with frigates and other armed vessels, which will always find security against a superior naval force in Elizabeth River."

APPENDIX.

NUMBER XI. Vide p. 7. l. 15.

Extract from Sir Henry Clinton's Letters to Lord George Germain.

OCTOBER 30, 1780. "I shall in a few days send to Charles-town, all the recruits belonging to the southern army, which will be about eight hundred. And then, including the corps under General Leslie, Lord Cornwallis will have full 11306 effective rank and file under his orders.

April 5th, 1781. "After the reduction of Charles-town, Lord Cornwallis informed me, that he thought the force I left with him fully competent to the defence of South, and most probably the reduction of North Carolina. I had, therefore, at that time no other intention (threatened as we were, by the expected arrival of a French fleet and army in Rhode-Island) than to send an expedition into Chesapeak, merely by way of making a diversion

diversion in his Lordship's favour, until more solid operation might take place. Which I was in hopes that adequate reinforcements from Europe, would have enabled me to undertake early in the present year. Events, however, notwithstanding the very glorious exertions which were made at Camden, altered Lord Cornwallis's situation so much as to make it necessary for him to call the corps I had sent to Chesapeak with General Leslie, (and which I had put under his Lordship's orders) to a nearer co-operation. Being, therefore, still desirous to secure a post in that bay to cover the King's frigates which might be acting there; and at the same time wishing to give Lord Cornwallis every assistance in my power; I sent thither another detachment, under the orders of Brigadier-general Arnold; which, though not so considerable as the former met with the fullest success, and will, I doubt not, have greatly aided the movements of the army in Carolina.

lina. General Washington having detached a body of troops to the southward, and the French having embarked in their fleet, another from their army at Rhode-island, with an apparent intention of interrupting our operations in Virginia, and the Carolinas; I was induced to send to the Chesapeak another expedition (drawn principally from the elite of my army) under Major-general Phillips. All these several detachments, your Lordship will perceive are acting, either with or in favour of Lord Cornwallis. But, as General Washington's letter to Mr. Harrison (a copy of which your Lordship will see amongst the intercepted letters inclosed) intimates, that there will not be opposed to his Lordship, above two thousand continentals more than General Green had with him before; I am led to hope that, when his Lordship has established himself in North-Carolina, a very confiderable portion of his army may be spared to assist in carrying into execution

execution such further operations, as Lord Cornwallis may have to propose; or the whole or such part as shall be found practicable of those I had designed, and accordingly explained to Major-general Phillips, in some conversations I had with him before his departure.

"If an attempt upon the forts in the high lands shall not, on mature deliberation, be thought adviseable, and nothing else offers in this quarter; I shall probably reinforce Major-general Phillips, and direct him to carry on such operations as may most effectually favour those of Lord Cornwallis, until some plan can be determined on for the campaign. For, until I know his Lordship's success, the force he can, in consequence of it, spare from the Carolinas, and the certainty of the arrival of the six regiments intended to reinforce us, it will be impossible to decide finally upon it. Your Lordship will, however, see by the inclosed opinions, what were the operations I had

had planned for the enfuing campaign, upon the fuppofition, that Lord Cornwallis fucceeded in the Carolinas, and was able to fpare a confiderable force from thence. With the ten thoufand men I requefted, I fhould not have had a doubt of fuccefs. But in my prefent reduced ftate and profpects I dare not flatter myfelf with any. And if the French fhould ftill be reinforced, your Lordfhip will, I am perfuaded, judge our fituation to be even critical. For with regard to our efforts in the Chefapeak, your Lordfhip knows how much their fuccefs and even the fafety of the armament there, will depend upon our having a decided naval fuperiority in thefe feas. And I, therefore, cannot doubt that every precaution will be taken, to give me, at leaft, timely notice of the contrary being likely to happen; as my ignorance of fuch an event, might be moft fatal in its confequences.

The

"The reinforcement I afked for, was only what I judged to be barely adequate to the fervices required; and I moft sincerely wifh it had been poffible to have fent it in the full extent of numbers, and in the time I requefted. However, the prefent reduced ftate of General Wafhington, the little probability there is, I hope, of an augmentation to the French armament, and the certainty there is, I likewife hope, of the fix Britifh regiments, and one thoufand recruits joining me in a fhort time, together, with the expectation I have of Lord Cornwallis's fuccefs in Carolina, enabling him to fend me a confiderable reinforcement from thence, render the appearances of my fituation lefs critical. And I fhall, therefore, only add, my Lord, that while the King does me the honour, to truft me with the command of this army, I will employ it to the utmoft of my poor abilities, for the promoting his fervice;— taking the liberty, however, to reprefent (as I think

I think it my duty) what advantages may be obtained by an additional force, and what evils may be apprehended from the want of a sufficient one.

April 30, 1781. "Your Lordship will have seen in the paper I had the honour to send you in my last dispatch, what force I judged would be requisite for this service. Not less, my Lord, than 10,000 men rank and file, fit for duty, indeed I wish they could be more. But the inclosed returns will shew your Lordship that after leaving these posts to their present garrisons, and leaving 1000 men in the post in Elizabeth River (supposing it may not be found necessary to occupy another station) I shall not have quite 5000 men for it, unless the three battalions expected from the West Indies arrive in proper time and condition for service, or Lord Cornwallis should be able to spare from his defensive in Carolina (when he determines upon it) a considerable part of the

the army under his immediate command; which, however, his Lordship's letter of the 10th instant, gives me no hopes of, or indeed that he will even spare me the three regiments coming from Ireland.

"With these 5000, however, my Lord, I may possibly determine to risk, even by desultory movements, the trial of this experiment, should I find, the report given me of our friends in that country properly founded. If it succeeds as fully as our sanguine friends would persuade us to hope, we may possibly be able to maintain ourselves there with a small force; but if we are in a situation to give the experiment a fair trial, and it then fails, I shall, I confess, have little hopes afterwards of re-establishing order on this continent; which I am free to own I think can never be effected without the cordial assistance of numerous friends, &c.

[*Inclosed*

Inclofed in the above letter the following extracts from Sir Henry Clinton's letters to Major General Phillips.

April 26, 1781.

"Lord Cornwallis's arrival at Wilmington has confiderably changed the complexion of our affairs to the fouthward; and all operations to the northward muft probably give place to thofe in favour of his Lordfhip, which at prefent appear to require our more immediate attention. I know nothing of his Lordfhip's fituation, but what I have learnt from his letter to me of the 10th, which you have read. I had great hopes, before I received this letter that his Lordfhip would have been in a condition to fpare me a confiderable part of his army from Carolina for the operations in Chefapeak; but you will obferve from it, that inftead of fending any part of his prefent force thither, he propofes to detain a part of the reinforcement coming from Europe for his more fouthern operations, even though

though they should be defensive. I shall therefore take the opinions of the general officers near me, upon the present state of our affairs, and afterwards send you such a reinforcement from this army, as we may judge can be done with tolerable security to this post, at least, while we remain superior at sea.

April 30, 1781. To the same. "If Lord Cornwallis proposes no operation to you soon (that is, before the month of June) and you see none that will operate for him *directly*. I think the best *indirect* one in his favour will be what you and General Arnold have proposed to me in Number 10 of your joint letter of the 18th instant. The only risk you run is from a temporary superiority of the enemy at sea; it is, however, an important move, and ought, in my opinion, to be tried even with some risk. Give me timely information of your intended move, and if possible I will follow you into ——— with such a small reinforcement as I can at the time spare.

"If

"If the next packet does not fatisfy me in —— I fhall probably retire and leave the command to Lord Cornwallis; to whom it will be my advice to try the only experiment that in my opinion can operate, if the one in Carolina has failed. For as to Virginia, I know none which can reduce that province in one campaign.

"As you feemed to think, before you received Lord Cornwallis's letter that all direct operation in favour of his Lordfhip would ceafe by the end of May, &c. pray let me receive General Arnold's, and your opinion as foon as poflible; I confefs, I am not fanguine, but if the experiment can be tried without any other rifk than from the enemy's fuperiority at fea I fhould wifh to do it.

"Should Lord Cornwallis determine on a defenfive in the Carolinas, he furely cannot want any of the European reinforcement, and will of courfe, fend it to you, and all fuch other as fhall arrive; thus reinforced, if after leaving

leaving a sufficient garrison in Elizabeth River, you can proceed to —— I think we shall be in force to give this a fair trial; and I may leave you in the command there, unless things should take a more favourable turn in the Carolinas, and Lord Cornwallis's presence there be no longer necessary. For until they do, I should imagine he will not quit them.

N. B. These two letters with other dispatches fell into Lord Cornwallis's hands on General Phillips's death and were opened by his Lordship; and the expedition therein proposed recommended to his consideration.

APPENDIX.

NUMBER XII. Vide p. 37. l. 6.

Extracts from Sir Henry Clinton's Letters to Lord George Germain.

May 20, 1781.

"BUT should Lord Cornwallis persist in his intention of joining Major-general Phillips, as mentioned in his letter to that General Officer, I shall be under some apprehensions for every part of South Carolina, except Charles-town, and even for Georgia, unless the speedy arrival of the reinforcement expected from Europe, may enable the officer, commanding in South Carolina, to take post in force in some healthy station in the back country.

"May 22. Notwithstanding the purport of these letters, I am yet in hopes, from Lord Cornwallis's letter to me of the 24th, that his Lordship will not persist in attempting a junction with Major-general Phillips, as I am am apprehensive it may be attended with some risk, not only to his own corps, but to that of General Phillips, should that General Officer not have been joined in time by the reinforcement I have sent him. And I even have my doubts whether his Lordship's march to the northward will draw after him, as he expects, the rebel General Green; who, I fear, will endeavour either to invest Camden, or, by stationing himself between that place and Charlestown, render Lord Rawdon's situation very hazardous. I am therefore induced to flatter myself, that Lord Cornwallis, when he hears of Lord Rawdon's success against Green, will rather march into South Carolina either by the direct route of Cross Creek and Camden, or by that of George Town; or even by embarkation, though he should be obliged to leave his cavalry behind until vessels can be sent for them, than attempt the proposed junction with General Phillips in the way he mentions;

APPENDIX.   iii

tions; which I muſt freely own appears to me, for the reaſons I have ſtated, not only dangerous to both corps in the attempt, but replete with the worſt conſequences to our ſouthern Provinces in their preſent ſtate."

NUMBER XIII. Vide p. 37. l. 11.

Extracts from Sir Henry Clinton's Letters to Lord George Germain.

July 18, 1781. "The extracts from my correſpondence with Earl Cornwallis, which I have had the honour to tranſmit from time to time to your Lordſhip, will ſhew, that I left in Carolina a very fair proportion of my army, and ſuch as his Lordſhip thought ſufficient to ſecure South, and recover North Carolina. With what was left for me to act with in this quarter, I took the field immediately upon my arrival here. General Leſlie's

Leslie's expedition to the Chesapeak took place afterwards; and some unfortunate events in Carolina calling for still farther reinforcement and co-operation, soon reduced this part of my army to a defensive, almost as low in numbers as Sir William Howe left me in 1777. If our successes, therefore, in the southern Provinces have not answered your Lordship's expectations, it cannot, I am certain, be imputed either to the smallness of the numbers I left there, or the tardiness or scantiness with which I have since supplied the exigencies of that service. Though I am strongly impressed with the importance of recovering Virginia, I fear the entire reduction of so populous a province is not to be expected from an operation solely there; unless our friends in it were more numerous, and were heartily inclined to assist us not only in conquering, but in keeping it.

July

APPENDIX.

July 25. "No man, my Lord, laments more sincerely than I do, the long continuance of the westerly winds, which prevented the sailing of the Warwick's convoy; and I hope your Lordship will pardon me for again repeating, that had the reinforcement sailed as early as was promised, and the three battalions not been detained in the West Indies, I should perhaps by this time have made such movements as would have obliged the enemy to be apprehensive for their own possessions, instead of meditating the attack which they now threaten against this post."

August 9. "I am entirely of your Lordship's sentiments with respect to Lord Cornwallis having done as much in North Carolina as could have been effected with his force. But I have to lament the causes which reduced it so low in number; and that his Lordship was induced to persist in his plan, after it became obvious that he was not able to establish himself there, and support and arm the Loyalists, which were the objects of his march into the heart of that province."

From Lord Cornwallis's former letters, I had every reason to suppose he thought himself in sufficient strength to command the success he hoped for. Had his Lordship, however, upon Lieutenant-colonel Tarleton's misfortune, called upon me for a reinforcement, or had I even known it in time, I am persuaded your Lordship will do me the justice to acknowledge, that it was absolutely out of my power to assist him more than I did; especially when it is considered, that at this moment his Lordship has acting with him, and in the different posts under his command, nineteen British, eight German, and fourteen Provincial battalions, besides detachments from four British battalions, and Iagers, artillery and cavalry; whilst in my present threatened situation, I have (through

(through my earnest desire to support his operations) left myself only eight British, eleven German, and four Provincial battalions, besides artillery and cavalry, for those in this quarter.

The END.

www.ingramcontent.com/pod-product-compliance
Lightning Source LLC
Chambersburg PA
CBHW020125170426
43199CB00009B/640